W9-BBX-112

Where in the World Can I . . .

BECOME A NINJA?

Where in the World Can I . . .

BECOME A NINJA?

WORLD BOOK

www.worldbook.com

World Book, Inc.
180 North LaSalle Street, Suite 900
Chicago, Illinois 60601
USA

For information about other World Book
publications, visit our website at
www.worldbook.com or call
1-800-WORLDBK (967-5325).

For information about sales to schools and
libraries, call 1-800-975-3250 (United States),
or 1-800-837-5365 (Canada).

Library of Congress Cataloging-in-Publication
Data for this volume has been applied for.

Where in the World Can I...
ISBN: 978-0-7166-2178-2 (set, hc.)

Become a Ninja?
978-0-7166-2179-9 (hc.)

Also available as:
978-0-7166-2189-8 (e-book)

Printed in China by Shenzhen Wing King Tong
Paper Products Co., Ltd., Shenzhen, Guangdong
1st printing July 2018

STAFF

Writer: Shawn Brennan

Executive Committee
President
 Jim O'Rourke

Vice President and
Editor in Chief
 Paul A. Kobasa

Vice President, Finance
 Donald D. Keller

Vice President, Marketing
 Jean Lin

Vice President,
International Sales
 Maksim Rutenberg

Vice President, Technology
 Jason Dole

Director, Human Resources
 Bev Ecker

Editorial
Director, New Print
 Tom Evans

Managing Editor, New Print
 Jeff De La Rosa

Senior Editor, New Print
 Shawn Brennan

Editor, New Print
 Grace Guibert

Librarian
 S. Thomas Richardson

Manager, Contracts &
Compliance (Rights &
Permissions)
 Loranne K. Shields

Manager, Indexing Services
 David Pofelski

Digital
Director, Digital Product
Development
 Erika Meller

Manager, Digital Products
 Jonathan Wills

Graphics and Design
Senior Art Director
 Tom Evans

Coordinator, Design
Development and
Production
 Brenda Tropinski

Media Researcher
 Rosalia Bledsoe

Manufacturing/
Production
Manufacturing Manager
 Anne Fritzinger

Proofreader
 Nathalie Strassheim

TABLE OF CONTENTS

WHAT IS A NINJA?

A *ninja (NIHN juh)* is a person who practices—does—*ninjutsu (nihn JUHT soo)*. Ninjutsu is a form of warfare that started long ago in Japan. Ninjutsu is part *espionage* (spying) and part *strategy*, or skillful planning, to reduce an enemy's military power. *Ninja* is a Japanese word that means "a person skilled in *stealth"* (secret action).

Ninja were often from Japan's lower social classes. They were masters at different kinds of *armed and unarmed combat* (fighting with and without weapons).

Ninja sometimes wore disguises and used poisons. Some people believed that ninja could even disappear! And some ninja were such great jumpers that people believed they could fly!

7

The military manual *The Art of War,* by the Chinese writer Sun Tzu (*suhn ZOO* or *suhn TSOO*), probably had something to do with the beginnings of ninjutsu. Sun Tzu lived around 500 B.C.

The book tells how to plan for war, how to fight battles, how to use the *terrain* (land surfaces) effectively, and how to make use of spies.

Prince Shotoku (*shoh TOH koo*) (573-621), a Japanese statesman and Buddhist scholar, may have been the first person to employ someone as a ninja. *Buddhism (BOO dihz uhm)* is one of the major religions of the world. It was started in India about 500 B.C. by a teacher called Buddha.

In 587, Shotoku used ninja to defeat a group of people who did not like Buddhists. Other people believe that the ninja started as a group of warrior priests called *yamabushi (YAH mah BOO shee)* who worshipped the mountains. By the 800's, ninja were *assassinating* (killing), kidnapping, and doing *sabotage (SAB uh tahzh)* (sneak damage).

Ninjutsu training developed mainly during the 1400's and 1500's. This was a time of great war in Japan. Ninja worked as assassins and gathered secret information for powerful families called *daimyo (DY myoh)* and warrior rulers called *shoguns (SHOH guhnz)*. Ninjutsu became organized into schools. Its *techniques* and *methods,* or ways and plans of doing things, were taught in a system. People think that there were once 49 schools of ninjutsu in Japan.

The two most well-known ninjutsu schools developed in Iga *(EE gah)*, in what is today Mie *(mee AY)* Prefecture (political unit), and nearby Koka *(KOH kah)* (also spelled Koga *[KOH gah]*), in what is today Shiga *(SHEE gah)* Prefecture. These places were surrounded by mountains and hard to reach. This helped keep ninjutsu training secret. Iga and Koka were still within reach of Kyoto *(kee OH toh)*, Japan's political center at the time.

Children born into the Iga and Koka ninja organizations were trained early as spies. Most began their training as young as age 6 or 7. The ninja continued in their craft for the rest of their lives.

11

After Japan became a unified nation in the 1600's, ninja began to scatter throughout the country and disappear. During the 1700's, the Japanese mostly used the word *shinobi (shih NOH bee)* to refer to "a person of stealth."

Both *ninja* and *shinobi* describe spies, scouts, and others who use stealthy methods for *paramilitary* purposes. A paramilitary warrior is not a member of the official armed forces of a country. Such warriors also do not follow the rules of warfare.

Shinobi and ninja used techniques and methods based on the *philosophy* of *ninpo (nihn POH)*. Philosophy is a study of ideas about how to live. *Ninpo* means "universal law of perseverance and endurance." *Perseverance* means sticking to an aim. *Endurance* is the power to keep on going no matter how hard something is to do. Ninpo told that spies and scouts did not follow the same rules as *samurai (SAM u ry)* and their servants. Samurai were the warrior class in Japan. But some ninja were also samurai and some samurai were trained in ninjutsu.

Ninja and samurai fought many battles against each other!

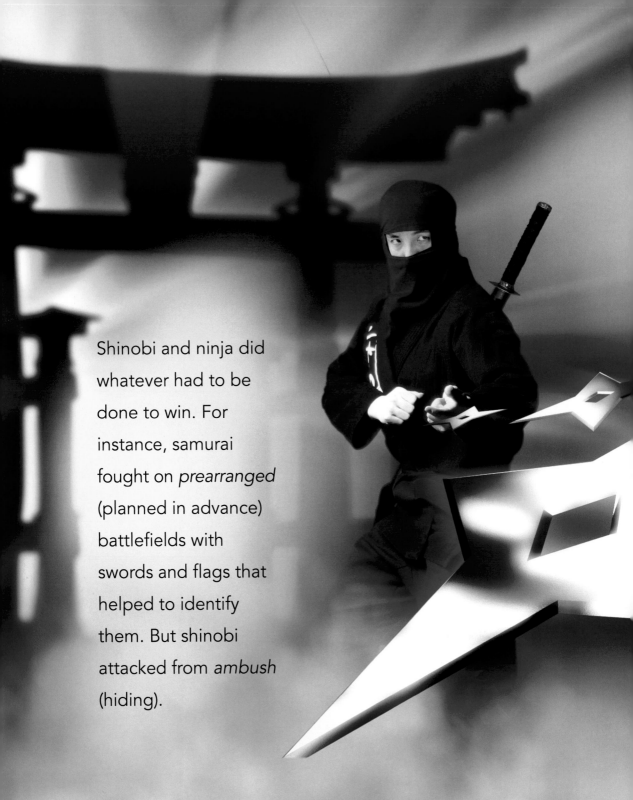

Shinobi and ninja did whatever had to be done to win. For instance, samurai fought on *prearranged* (planned in advance) battlefields with swords and flags that helped to identify them. But shinobi attacked from *ambush* (hiding).

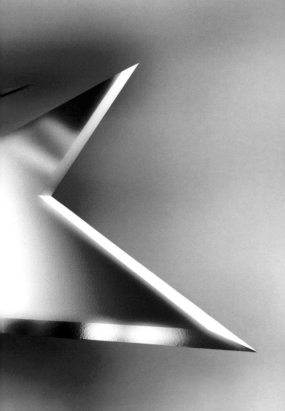

Shinobi used knives, bladed throwing discs or stars, called *shuriken (shoo REE kehn)*, and other carefully hidden weapons. Shinobi and ninja also hired themselves out to anyone who could pay for their services.

The code of the samurai called for the warrior to die with honor. But the code of the shinobi allowed a person to sneak away and hide in buildings or bushes. The shinobi had a strict code of silence. He never revealed his name, *objective* (goal), or techniques—even to the point of death! If a ninja or shinobi was about to be captured, rather than be tortured to death, he either killed himself or was killed by another ninja.

15

Women called kunoichi *(koo NOY chee)* were also an important part of shinobi *clans,* or groups. The kunoichi's beauty and charm were her main weapons! Kunoichi often posed as performers or servants in the homes of enemies. In these disguises, kunoichi sneaked into temples, castles, and fortresses. They gathered information from well-protected targets shinobi could not reach!

But a kunoichi did use such weapons as poisons and shuriken to keep her distance from the enemy. If she was discovered, a kunoichi might use her *neko-te (NEH koh TAY)* or *cat hands.* These were leather finger sheaths topped with sharp metal "claws." These weapons were long and sharp enough to tear into skin!

16

Today, a female ninja or woman that practices ninjutsu martial arts is often called a kunoichi.

17

Ninja have often been featured in Japanese puppet plays, theatrical productions, and woodblock prints. The ninja were dressed in all black. This was done to let the audience know that the ninja could not be seen by people in the scene with the warrior.

More recently, ninja have also appeared in novels, films, *anime (A nee may)*, and video games. Anime is a type of cartoon animation that developed in Japan. The ninja are usually shown as martial *(MAHR shuhl)* arts experts dressed in black clothes. Martial arts are fighting arts.

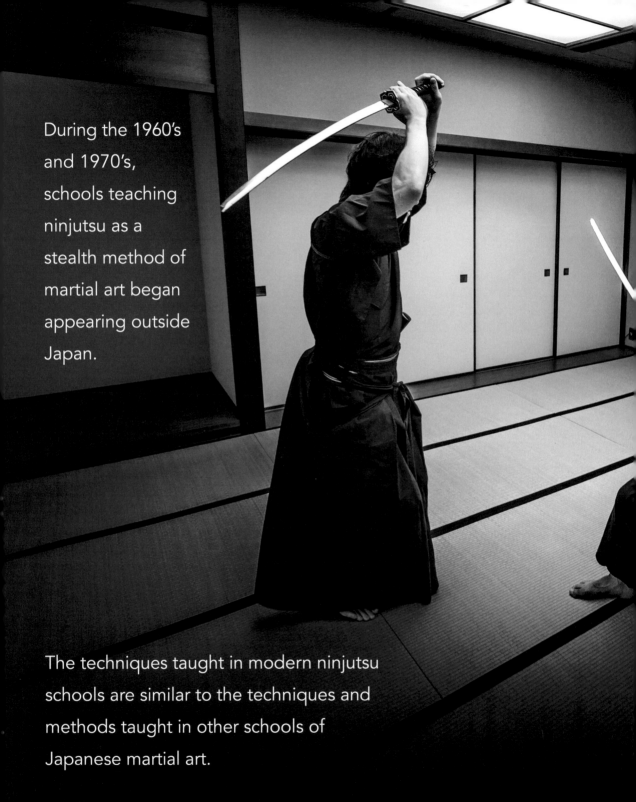

During the 1960's and 1970's, schools teaching ninjutsu as a stealth method of martial art began appearing outside Japan.

The techniques taught in modern ninjutsu schools are similar to the techniques and methods taught in other schools of Japanese martial art.

Today, there are many places around the world where you can train to become a ninja martial artist.

Do you think you have what it takes to become a modern-day ninja? Find out as we visit the two places where ninjutsu all began!

IGA

In the tiny village of Akame (*ah KAH may*), in the Iga region of Japan, you can experience the training of Iga ninja as if you were a warrior in the 1400's! Ninja Training Forest at Akame 48 Waterfalls recreates some of the ways that ninja learned and practiced their skills. A string of beautiful waterfalls flows through the area. Iga ninja trained among these waterfalls. Here they practiced such skills as climbing and walking on slippery rocks and hiding behind the falling water! They even learned to make medicine and poisons from the plants that grew here.

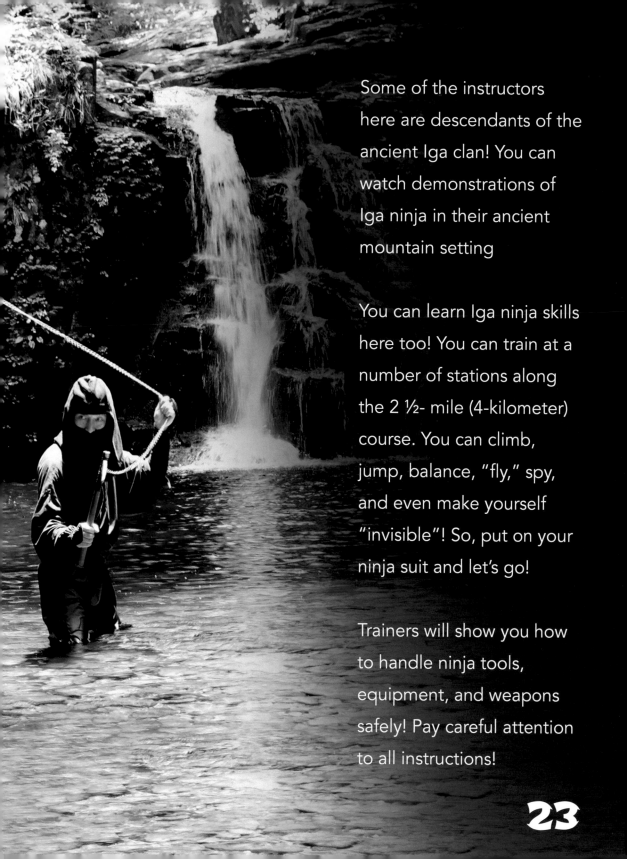

Some of the instructors here are descendants of the ancient Iga clan! You can watch demonstrations of Iga ninja in their ancient mountain setting

You can learn Iga ninja skills here too! You can train at a number of stations along the 2 ½- mile (4-kilometer) course. You can climb, jump, balance, "fly," spy, and even make yourself "invisible"! So, put on your ninja suit and let's go!

Trainers will show you how to handle ninja tools, equipment, and weapons safely! Pay careful attention to all instructions!

The training begins with the humming of the *kuji-kiri (KOO jee KEE ree)*. Nine hand gestures go along with the humming. This helps increase mental concentration and energy. The gestures also help build hand strength.

Each hand gesture symbolizes a different ability that the ninja may call upon.

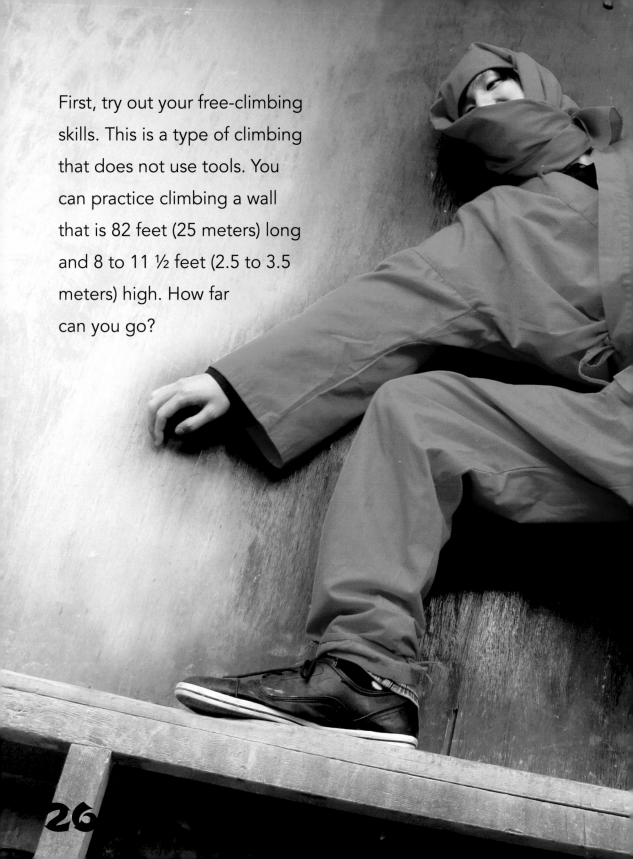

First, try out your free-climbing skills. This is a type of climbing that does not use tools. You can practice climbing a wall that is 82 feet (25 meters) long and 8 to 11 ½ feet (2.5 to 3.5 meters) high. How far can you go?

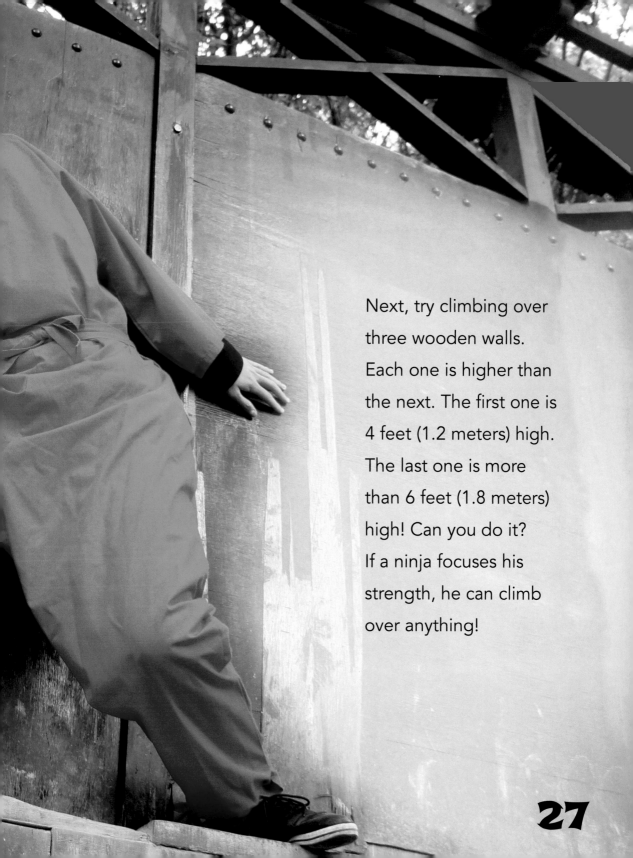

Next, try climbing over three wooden walls. Each one is higher than the next. The first one is 4 feet (1.2 meters) high. The last one is more than 6 feet (1.8 meters) high! Can you do it? If a ninja focuses his strength, he can climb over anything!

Now practice your intrusion
(ihn TROO zhuhn) techniques!
Intrusion means entering
without being asked.

The ninja flung a rope across one rooftop to
another and quickly shimmied across it on his
stomach. Can you shimmy across a 50-foot-
(15-meter-) long rope strung between two trees?
Use your legs to help keep your balance!

You can try walking across a flat rope that is 50 feet (15 meters) long and 2 inches (5 centimeters) wide. Sharpen your senses like a ninja to make it across!

Can you fly like a ninja? Do the flying ape and swing from tree to tree! A cord will help you swing far.

Do the raccoon dog! Learn how to climb a tree and hide behind it to make yourself invisible to enemies! Ninja were able to climb up tall, smooth tree trunks in order to look over the landscape around them.

Climb a wall using special ropes and sickles! With the right tools, ninja could even climb up castle walls!

Do the ninja walk across a log! Ninja could walk on the edge of a wall or rooftop without making a sound!

Learn how to throw four-
and eight-pointed steel
shuriken at the enemy!
Ninja must know how to
target vital body parts.
Throw the shuriken while
you fly away!

Use the *fugue (fyoog)*
technique to vanish
through hidden doors
and escape through
holes!

Practice stealth like a
ninja! Learn how to open
a hole in the wall or the
floor to spy and enter a
house!

Foil your enemies in the dark! Use the *katana (kah TAH nah)*, a traditional long, curved sword to find enemies and knock them down in a single strike.

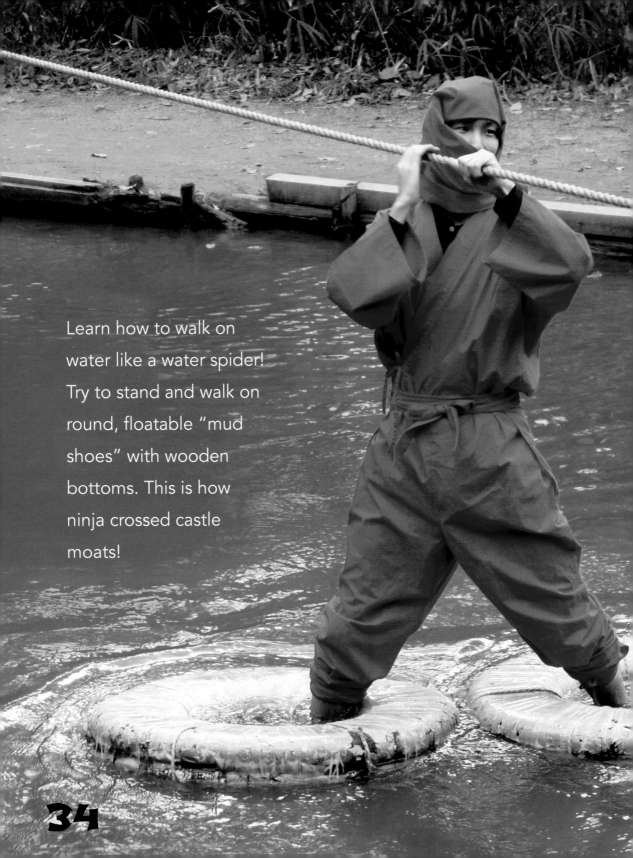

Learn how to walk on water like a water spider! Try to stand and walk on round, floatable "mud shoes" with wooden bottoms. This is how ninja crossed castle moats!

34

At the end of your training, you will receive a ninja scroll certificate of completion!

Congratulations!

Japanese characters for ninja

About 17 miles (27 kilometers) north of Akame is the Iga Ueno *(EE gah oo EH noh)* Castle.

It is often called the White Phoenix *(FEE nihks)* because it resembles the mythical bird called the phoenix, sitting in a nest. The castle was built in the 1500's. It is perched on a hill overlooking the town.

The castle was built under the command of Takigawa Katsutoshi *(tah kee GAH wah KAT soo TOH shee)*. Katsutoshi was the shogun who ruled this area at the time. He used ninja for spying into political matters. Today, the castle contains a display of samurai weapons and armor, scrolls, artwork, and *artifacts* (things made by people) from around the region. The castle is registered as a National Historical Site.

Down the hill from the Iga Ueno Castle is the Iga Ninja Museum. It was built in 1964 to showcase the history of the Iga ninja. First, you can explore a recreated ninja house. This is a real ninja house that was moved from a nearby place and rebuilt here. A kunoichi guides you through each part of the house. This simple farm house features revolving doors, hidden rooms, and secret exits. This way ninja could escape intruders and keep weapons safe.

The museum's Ninja Tradition Hall explains how ninja trained and fought. You will learn how ninja navigated, using the stars at night and shadows cast by sticks during the day. You will also learn how ninja could tell the time by looking at a cat's eyes! At the Ninja Experience Hall, you can watch a video of Iga ninja sneaking into Ueno Castle!

At Ninja Experience Ground, you can see a live show of ninja demonstrating ancient weapons, such as swords, shuriken, and the *kusarigama* (*ksah ree GAH muh* or *koo SAH ree GAH muh*)—a metal chain with a long, curved blade at the end.

39

KOKA

About 14 miles (23 kilometers) north of Iga Ueno Castle, you can visit the last real ninja house in Japan! It stands in the place where it was built—in Koka, the other important place where ninjutsu developed.

The Koka Ninja House was built over 300 years ago. It was the home of Mochizuki Izumonokami *(MOH chee ZOO kee IHZ oo moh noh KAH mee)*, the head of the Koka ninja clan at that time. It looks like an ordinary house from the outside. But inside, there are many traps and devices to keep out intruders and to provide a means of quick and stealthy escape. Visitors are allowed to explore the house and discover its various trapdoors and secret passages.

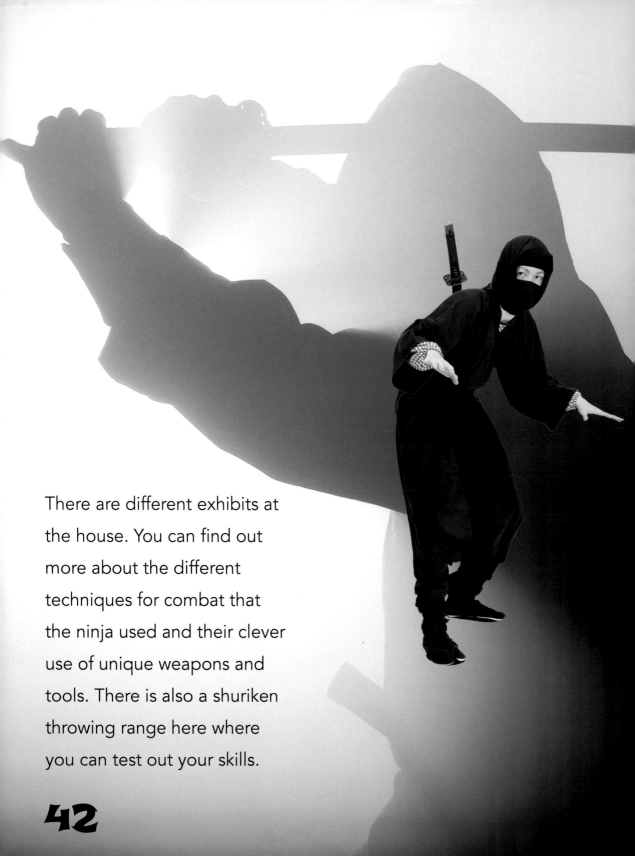

There are different exhibits at the house. You can find out more about the different techniques for combat that the ninja used and their clever use of unique weapons and tools. There is also a shuriken throwing range here where you can test out your skills.

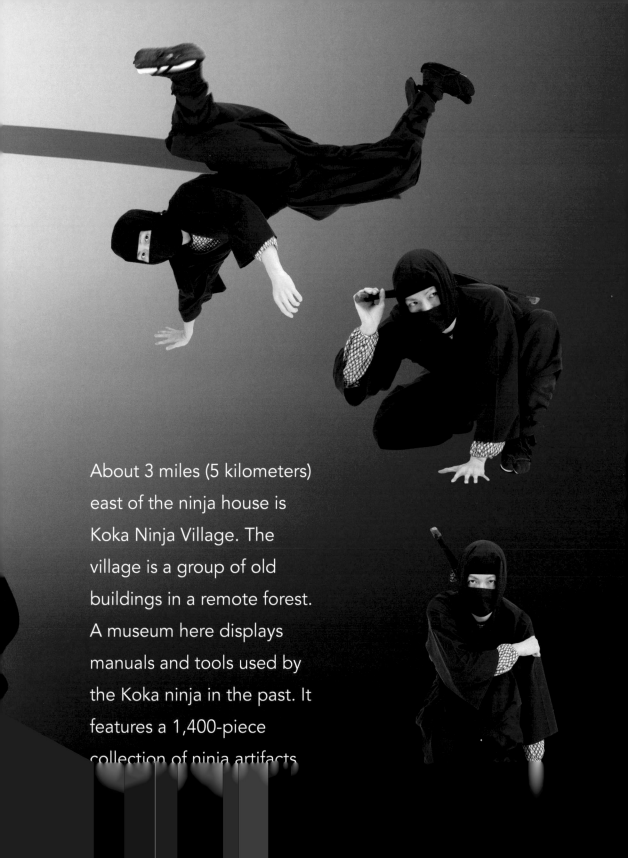

About 3 miles (5 kilometers) east of the ninja house is Koka Ninja Village. The village is a group of old buildings in a remote forest. A museum here displays manuals and tools used by the Koka ninja in the past. It features a 1,400-piece collection of ninja artifacts.

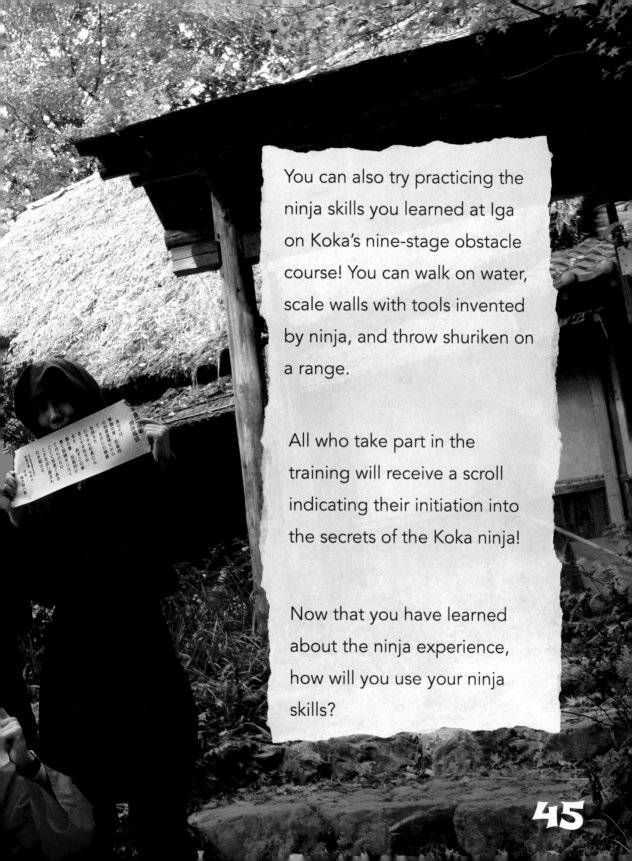

You can also try practicing the ninja skills you learned at Iga on Koka's nine-stage obstacle course! You can walk on water, scale walls with tools invented by ninja, and throw shuriken on a range.

All who take part in the training will receive a scroll indicating their initiation into the secrets of the Koka ninja!

Now that you have learned about the ninja experience, how will you use your ninja skills?

BOOKS AND WEBSITES

BOOKS

Ninja by Sean McDaniel (Bellwether Media, 2011)
In this book, students will learn about the history, training, and techniques that made ninja deadly warriors.

Ninja by Jim Ollhoff (ABDO, 2008)
This volume in the "World of Martial Arts" series explores the world of the ninja, weaving together history, culture, geography, and politics.

Ninjas by Rupert Matthews (Gareth Stevens, 2015)
This volume in the "History's Fearless Fighters" series details what is known about ninja training, disguises, weapons, and reputation. Includes a timeline overview of the rise and fall of the ninja.

You Wouldn't Want to Be a Ninja Warrior! A Secret Job That's Your Destiny by John Malam (Scholastic, 2012)
This illustrated volume describes how tough life could be for ninja in feudal Japan, then sends readers on an exciting, covert mission to steal an enemy warlord's plans.

WEBSITES

Koka Ninja House Website
http://www.kouka-ninjya.com/la_en/

Official website of the Koka Ninja House. Includes visitor information as well as articles and information on the history of the Koka and Iga ninja.

Ninja Museum of Igaryu
https://www.iganinja.jp/en/exp/intro.html

Official website of the Ninja Museum of Igaryu. Includes sections on the history of ninja and ninjutsu, information on ninja training in Japan, ninjutsu preservation, descriptions of nearby sites to visit that are connected with Japan's ninja history, and Iga travel information.

Way of Ninja
https://www.wayofninja.com/where-can-i-learn-ninjutsu/

This website includes sections on how to be a ninja in real life, including mental and physical training and "street know-how." It also features articles about ninja and samurai history, culture, and folklore in Japan.

INDEX

ACKNOWLEDGMENTS

Cover: © Fotokvadrat/Shutterstock; © 1001 Nights/ iStockphoto

2-5 © Shutterstock

6-7 © Nicolas McComber, iStockphoto

8-9 *Moriya Pursuing Prince Shōtoku who Disappears into a Tree* (19th century), color woodblock print by Utagawa Kuniyoshi; Los Angeles County Museum of Art

10-11 © DeAgostini/Getty Images

12-15 © Shutterstock

16-17 © Everett Historical/Shutterstock; go.biwako (licensed under CC BY-SA 2.0)

18-19 Library of Congress

20-21 © Shutterstock

22-23 Photo by Geoff Day, Japantravel.com

24-25 © Vantherra/Adobe Stock

26-27 go.biwako (licensed under CC BY-SA 2.0)

28-29 © Shutterstock

30-31 From *Ninja III: The Domination* (© Cannon Films)

32-33 © Shutterstock

34-35 go.biwako (licensed under CC BY-SA 2.0)

36-39 © Shutterstock

40-41 Ōshima Takuya, Nippon.com

42-43 © Shutterstock

44-45 go.biwako (licensed under CC BY-SA 2.0); © STILLFX/Shutterstock